Cycling in Ho

An e-pocket gu

Produced by www.holidaysbycycle.com

2016

In association with

Contents

"You can't buy happiness, but you can buy a bicycle and that's pretty close."

About this e-pocket guide

This e-pocket guide serves as a brief introduction to holiday cycling in Holland pinpointing the key resources on the net and offering a few destination and route suggestions. Although useful in hard copy format, this guide is designed primarily for use on portable internet enabled devices. By utilising hyperlinks, the reader can be directed to more in depth information as and when they feel is necessary, making the guide simple, efficient and relevant to your needs. The handful of "recommended" routes, places, accommodation…and so forth, have been selected on the basis of research, recommendation, and occasionally, personal experience. As such, the information is provided in good faith and we cannot always guarantee the accuracy, and welcome any feedback that will improve and develop the guides in the future (info@holidaysbycycle.com). The individual guides in this series will form the basis of a wider compilation covering some of the best countries to cycle in Europe.

About Holidays by Cycle

Holidays by Cycle (www.holidaysbycycle.com) is a non-profit social enterprise and registered Community Interest Company (CIC) set up to promote cycle tourism in Europe by linking related services. The rationale behind the project is that by doing so, this low carbon form of slow travel will become more accessible to the "general" tourist and help reduce the reliance on cars. Holiday cycling is a fast growing niche of tourism, and our mission is to help make this activity a mainstream option for anyone planning a vacation. On the Holidays by Cycle website you can find a selection of the best organised tours in Europe, cycle friendly accommodation in over 20 countries, cycle hire in 600 locations and some route suggestions - as well as find information on city cycling and places of interest. You can read more about us at the end of this guide.

"Whenever I see an adult on a bicycle, I do not despair for the human race." HG Wells, English author

Holiday cycling in Holland: the basics

Overview

Holland has been a cyclist's paradise for many years, consistently leading the way in terms of integrating cycling into mainstream society. The country is regularly regarded as one of the best places to cycle in Europe, owing to its cycle friendly infrastructure, lack of hills, temperate climate and widespread cultural embrace this model of transport has enjoyed. Statistics embarrass many other European countries, with cycling accounting for 27% of all journeys taken nationwide and 38% in the capital city Amsterdam (I Amsterdam 2015). Indeed Amsterdam, otherwise known as "the city of bikes", is synonymous with cycling, being one of the world's leading "cycle cities", and its alternative culture, unique identity and hectic cosmopolitan feel makes it one of the most visited cities in Europe. Rotterdam and The Hague are also great tourism destinations and both serve the cyclist well. Further afield the peaceful countryside rewards you with tulip fields and windmills readily accessible through its well-designed and signed network of cycle routes totalling almost 35,000km. Consequently, as a destination for holiday cycling, the Netherlands is always a serious consideration.

Taken from: www.holland.com

National organisations and general information

Given the emphasis on cycling in the country, it is no surprise that finding quality cycle tourism related information is relatively easy and the internet is awash with resources. A good starting point is Nederland Fietsland (www.nederlandfietsland.nl), part of Landelijk Fietsplatform the official Dutch organisation for recreational cycling. Their website is clear, concise and full of useful information directed at the tourist, such as short and long routes, an online route planner, accommodation, maps and guides. Similarly, the Dutch Cyclists Union (www.fietsersbond.nl/) offer a wealth of detailed information and a user friendly route planner. Both the Nederland Fietsland and Fietserbond route planners allow you to type in your route preferences and populate an interactive map with suggestions tailored to your requirements, as well as showing local cycle friendly resources such as accommodation and places to eat. Other recommended sources of information specific to cycling in Holland are the internet guides Holland-Cycling.com (www.holland-cycling.com) and Cycling in the Netherlands (www.holland.cyclingaroundtheworld.nl). The sites cover route and holiday suggestions, city guides, planning, tips and advice and are both compiled with care and dedication by informed cyclists.

The cycle network

The cycle routes in Holland are varied and well sign posted. Shorter routes or day trips include the *junction routes*, which cover the entire country. This system is incredibly well organised and consists of junction points with unique reference numbers and detailed information about other connecting local routes and their corresponding distances. This gives the cyclist a number of options to continue their journey, enabling the nature of the route and its length to be tailored. There are also a number of themed routes, usually around 40km long, that utilise the wider network, such as the Mill Route and the Ferry Route. For longer distances the national LF routes (landelijke fietsroutes) are ideal with the entire network covering around 4500km. Again these are well sign posted and often cross boarders into neighbouring countries or make up international routes such as EuroVelo 15 (The Rhine Cycle Route). All route types interlink and the network is comprehensively mapped on the online route planners provided by www.nederlandfietsland.nl and www.fietsersbond.nl.

Finding a place to stay

In terms of accommodation, cyclists are well catered for with a national network of cycling friendly accommodation regulated by Holland's cyclist welcome scheme (www.allefietserswelkom.nl), and there is a general acceptance of cyclists in wider accommodation. Cyclists welcome accommodation is varied, from hotels to campsites, and all National Park Campsites (www.natuurkampeerterreinen.nl) are members of the scheme. For budget accommodation the Hikers Huts (www.trekkershutten.nl) are a good option, offering simple log cabins with bunk beds sleeping 4/5 from 37 euro per night. Another useful budget option is the Friends of Cyclists network (www.vriendenopdefiets.nl) which offers a list of non-commercial accommodation from just 19 euro per person per night. Other options include Stayokay (www.stayokay.com) who are part of Youth Hostelling International, and bedandbreakfast.nl (www.bedandbreakfast.nl) which lists B&B's across the country. Helpfully, Cyclist Welcome accommodation is also mapped on the route planners provided by Nederland Fietsland (www.nederlandfietsland.nl) and the Dutch Cyclists Union (www.fietsersbond.nl/).

"Melancholy is incompatible with bicycling." James E Starrs

Regions and places: some recommendations

De Hoge Veluwe Park

Hoge Veluwe National Park (www.hogeveluwe.nl) is located in the province of Gelderland and comprises 5,400 hectares of woodland, heathland, drift sands and peat bogs. Amongst these varied habitats can be found an array of fauna and flora, and populations of Red Dear, Boar, Roe and Corsican Sheep roam its fenced perimeters. The park also has some impressive buildings such as St Hubertus Hunting Lodge and the Kroller-Muller Museum, showcasing important pieces from artists such as Picasso, Rodin and Van Gogh. The park is privately run as a foundation and its upkeep is dependant on paying visitors, with a daily rate of 8.80 euro for adults and 4.40 euro for children.

The park operates a bike share system with a fleet of "White Bicycles" that can be used to cycle the 40km of dedicated paths within the park. The White Bicycles are an intrinsic part of the park and are the primary means of getting around. The Park has a total of 1,700 White Bikes and they are all free to use. The bikes are located at various storage facilities at the Marchantplein, the Kröller-Müller Museum, Jachthuis Sint Hubertus and the Hoenderloo, Otterlo and Schaarsbergen entrances. Children's Bikes and bicycles with child seats are also available. You can, of course, use your own bikes around the park or hire bikes from outside the park.

Taken from: www.hogeveluwe.nl

It is possible to camp within the park and a campsite is located at the Hoenderloo entrance. The site is car free, and a tent pitch for the night is 7 euro per person (2015). For accommodation outside the park there are a number of "Cyclists Welcome" certified options that include: **Hotel Papendal** (www.papendal.com Papendallaan 3, 6816 VD, Arnhem), **Hotel Vierhouten** (www.hotelvierhouten.nl Tongerenseweg 1, 8076 PV, Vierhouten), **Camping De Wije Werelt** (www.ardoer.com/en/camping/wije-werelt Arnhemseweg 100-102, 6731 BV, Otterlo) and **Camping Beek en Hei** (www.campingbeekenhei.nl Heideweg 4, 6731 SN, Otterlo).

Dutch Wadden Sea Islands

The Dutch Wadden Sea Islands (www.waddensea-worldheritage.org) consist of five varied pearls nestled in the sea north of Holland and make up part of the Wadden Sea world heritage site. The islands are part of a larger archipelago that stretches as far as Denmark and consists of a number of environmentally diverse and protected habitats.

Taken from: Openstreetmap

The islands, Schiermonnikoog, Ameland, Terschelling, Vlieland and Texel, are easy to access from the mainland and connecting ferries make island hoping by bike relatively straight forward. Schiermonnikoog (www.schiermonnikoog.info) has been voted the prettiest place in the Netherlands by Dutch people with its picturesque houses and long beaches the primary attraction. Ameland is famous for its traditional "commander houses" which used to house the captains of the whale hunting boats. An arts festival each November is another draw. At Terschelling (www.terschelling.org) you can visit the town of West Terschelling and see the pretty marina with around 450 moored boats. The sandy and wild Island of Vlieland (www.vlieland-info.nl and www.vlieland.org) has a calm atmosphere with car use limited to locals. Each year Vlieland hosts several events, including a music festival in September. Texel (www.texel.net) is the largest of the Dutch Wadden Islands and is busy all year with activities and events. The island has a nature centre and seal reserve and hosts a popular food festival in September.

For cyclists the Islands offer a relatively flat terrain, varied landscapes and a peaceful retreat away from cars, pollution and hustle. Ferries allow you to hop between the islands, taking in the various events, historic buildings, wide open beaches and dramatic scenery as you travel. The islands are renowned for their cycle friendly attributes and attract all levels of cyclist, and for the more dedicated, the Islands make up part of the longer North Sea Cycle Route so can be incorporated into longer cycling tours. Two good "day" cycle rides around Texel can be found in the *Day trip* section of Holland-Cycling.com (www.holland-cycling.com).

Cycle hire outlets are numerous, and bike hire companies are often listed on the islands dedicated websites. Cycle hire providers include: **Vermeulen Bikes** (www.vermeulenbikes.nl Herenstraat 69, 1797 AG, Den Hoorn, Texel), **Solexverhuur Texel** (www.solexverhuurtexel.nl Postweg 79, 1795 JK, de Cocksdorp, Texel), **Fiets Inn Texel** (www.fietsinn-texel.nl Nikadel 75 1796 BR De Koog, Texel), **Zeelen Fietsverhuur** (www.zeelenfiets.nl Voor al uw vragen, Telefoon, Terschelling and also available on Vlieland), **Rijwielverhuur Tijsknop** (www.tijsknop.nl Torenstraat 10-12, West Terschelling, Terschelling), **Jan Van Vlieland** (www.janvanvlieland.nl Havenweg 7, 8899 BB, Vlieland) and **Fietsenverhuur Soepboer** (www.fietsenverhuurschiermonnikoog.com Paaslandweg 1, 9166 PV, Schiermonnikoog)

Accommodation can be found on all the Dutch Wadden Sea islands and can range from campsites to hotels and listings can be found on the islands individual websites. Certified cyclists welcome accommodation includes: **Klif 1 B&B** (www.klif1.nl Klif 1, 1797 AK, Den Hoorn, Texel); **Hotel Den Burg** (www.hoteldenburg.nl Emmalaan 2-4, 1791 AV, Den Burg, Texel) and **Boerderijcamping Anemoonè** (www.anemoone.nl Maaikeduinweg 10, 1796 MN, De Koog, Texel), **Hotelletje de Veerman** (www.hotelletjedeveerman.nl Dorpsstraat 173, 8899 AG, Oost-Vlieland); **Hotel DoniaState** (www.doniastatevlieland.nl Badweg 2, 8899 BV, Vlieland) and **Staatsbosbeheer Nature Reserve** in the centre of Vlieland offers camping facilities (www.staatsbosbeheer.nl).

"Life is like riding a bicycle. In order to keep your balance, you must keep moving." Albert Einstein

The River Vecht

Winding its way majestically between Amsterdam and Utrecht, the river Vecht makes the perfect, tranquil cycle route. The countryside along this river, in particular the 35km between Weesp and Utrecht, is characterised by quiet lanes, country mansions (built with the wealth of Dutch merchants), castles and scenic vistas. The river itself makes up the LF16 Vecht Valley Route that stretches for 230km from Zwolle to Darfeld in Germany. Some particularly interesting towns on route include monument-packed Breukelen - a town with a name that's known as far away as America (Breukelen becoming Brooklyn after Dutch immigrants settled there in the 17th century). Further down the Vecht are the towns of Loenen and Vreeland, two lovely old towns with notable architectural heritage.

Taken from: www.holland.com

Of particular interest is the town of Utrecht (www.visit-utrecht.com). This lively and beautiful university town has plenty to see and is dominated by the impressive 14th century Dom tower. The car free centre is steeped in history, and has an attractive network of canals to explore. So beautiful is this majestic town, that it has been described by In your Pocket as "Netherlands' most charming city" (www.inyourpocket.com).

Utrecht has no shortages of cafes, restaurants and places to visit, and is in the running to become European Capital of Culture in 2018.

Cycle Cities

Amsterdam

Given that Amsterdam is known as "the city of bikes", it is no surprise this fascinating and vibrant city is not only the best city to cycle in Holland, but also one of the best in Europe. Amsterdam has around 400km of bicycle paths crossing the city, and it has been estimated that half the journeys in the city take place on a bike. Bike culture is everywhere, and a trip to Amsterdam is not complete without a cycle trip or two. If the hustle and bustle of the city is too much to cope with then it's easy to escape the crowds and cycle to the Metropolitan areas, and in just over an hour you could be arriving in Waterland or Muiden, and the historic city of Muiderslot.

Amsterdam has an official tourist website I Amsterdam (www.iamsterdam.com) which covers every aspect of tourism in the city, and has a dedicated and well-informed section on cycling from which you can find information on cycle hire, routes and tours.

As with other cities in Holland, there is no dedicated bike share scheme in Amsterdam. This may seem surprising, but is generally down to the fact 40% of residents in Amsterdam own a bike and a public bike share system is simply not justified - although plans are underway to introduce a scheme aimed at tourists. However, the national OV Fiets system (www.ov-fiets.nl) serves the city well with a number of hire locations around the city and within Central Train Station. The system is generally geared towards residents and requires a yearly subscription, but for regular visitors this system is well worth considering. Anyhow, independent cycle hire companies within the city are plentiful so finding a bike to hire is not a problem. These outlets supply a range of bikes to suit most scenarios, and many have been operating for many years so are really useful sources of local information. Many of these companies can be viewed on the I Amsterdam website (www.iamsterdam.com) and it is worth noting that some hire companies offer a 25% discount with an I Amsterdam City Card (see the I Amsterdam website for information on the benefits of this card). Cycle hire providers include: **Discount Bike Rental** (www.discountbikerental.nl Nieuwe Nieuwstraat 19, 1012, Amsterdam) located near Central station and offering 24 hour hire for around 8.50 euro; **Amstel Fietspoint** (www.amstelfietspoint.nl ulianaplein 1, 1097 DN, Amsterdam) located near Amstel train station; **Macbike Vondelpark** (www.macbike.nl Overtoom 45 1054 HB Amsterdam), operating for over 25 years and offers a 25% discount with I Amsterdam City Card; **Bike City** (www.bikecity.nl Bloemgracht 68-70 1015 TL Amsterdam), located in Jordaan area; **Rent a Bike Haarlem** (www.rentabikehaarlem.nl Lange Herenstraat 36 2011 LJ Haarlem), great location near station and 25% discount with I Amsterdam City Card.

"Learn to ride a bicycle. You will not regret it if you live." Mark Twain, American author and humourist

The Hague

The Hague is Holland's third largest city and, as you may expect, one of the best cities to cycle in Europe. The relatively compact size and dedicated cycle paths make cycling an attractive way to see the sites. The Hague is renowned for its stately architecture, royal connections, historic centre and market squares and is often overlooked by tourists in favour of Amsterdam. As well as the attractions of the city centre, nearby towns such as Delft and the seaside resort of Scheveningen are within a cycling distance and there are some good cycle routes out of the city into surrounding countryside. The Hague has a really useful tourism website The Hague (www.denhaag.com) although specific cycling related information is difficult to find. Although there is a bike share scheme operating in The Hague under the national public bike transport system (www.ov-fiets.nl) this is geared more towards regular users and residents as it requires a subscription. However, a number of bike rental companies operating in and around The Hague that offer quality and affordable rental, and many of these are located at train stations making cycle-rail travel relatively simple. At The Hague Central station you will find **Rijwiel Shop** (www.rijwielshopdenhaag.nl) offering daily and weekly hire from 7.50 euro a day. Other hire options within the city include **Grote Markt** (www.biesieklette.nl), **Fietsverhuur Den Haag** (www.fietsverhuurdenhaag.nl) and **Rijwielshop Hollands Spoor** (www.rijwielshop-hollands-spoor.nl).

In terms of local routes, the online route planner provided by the Dutch Cyclist Association (www.fietsersbond.nl) is a good starting point. For some more specific route ideas Fietsersbond has produced Parkenroute, a detailed guide to three green routes in and around The Hague designed to connect parks and country estates. This guide can be purchased from the local tourist office or a PDF download in English can be found on The Hague official website (www.denhaag.nl/en/residents/to/Parkenroute-for-cyclists.htm). Outside of the city are some good day trip routes such as the Delft Cycle Route. This takes you from the historic centre of Delft to the wetlands of the Midden-Delftland region which sits between The Hague, Delft and Rotterdam. The route is well described in a Holland-Cycling.com PDF download (www.holland-cycling.com/assets/docs/DelftCycleRoute.pdf?) and the website has a dedicated section on The Hague where you will find a wealth of useful information about cycling in the region.

There are a number of cycle tour operators within the city offering a range of guided trips taking in city sites and the surrounding countryside. Themed tours include arts, architecture and royal residences. Tour operators include **City Cycle Tours** (www.citycycletours.nl), **Holland Tour Guides** (www.hollandtourguides.com), **One Day Bike Tours** (www.holland-onedaybiketours.nl) and **Totzo** (www.totzo.org).

The Hague offers a range of accommodation options to suit most budgets, from city centre hotels to campsites on the outskirts. Many offer bike hire, or have bike storage and several are members of the cyclist welcome scheme and can be found on the Fietsersbond route planner (www.fietsersbond.nl). Suggestions include **The student hotel** (www.thestudenthotel.com) which offers bike rental, **Court Garden Hotel** (www.hotelcourtgarden.nl) an eco-hotel with a dedicated bike store, **Hotel Petit: Best Western** (www.hotelpetit.nl) registered as cyclists welcome with bike hire and store and **Camping Duinhorst** (www.duinhorst.nl) a cyclist welcome campsite 5km from Hague.

Rotterdam

Rotterdam (www.rotterdam.info) is a city of contrasts; from the utilitarian harbour to the hip and trendy nightlife - there is plenty to offer every taste. Architecturally, the city has a dynamic skyline, boasting cutting edge skyscrapers, and culturally there are a number of fine museums such as the Chabot, Boijmans Van Beuningen and Kunstha, which between them showcase a range of local and international art as well as varied exhibitions.

From a cycling point of view, the city offers a great deal, with its typically Dutch approach to two wheeled transport. The city has an extensive network of cycle paths (an integral part of post war town planning) that extent beyond the metropolitan area, and services such as cycle hire and tours are easy to access.

Taken from: www.rotterdam.info

Rotterdam's main tourism site (www.rotterdam.info) offers some good general information on the city, but lacks a dedicated cycling area. More informative in this respect is City Guide Rotterdam (www.cityguiderotterdam.com) that offers a detailed page including tips and links on cycle hire, tours and routes. The Rotterdam page on www.holland-cycling.com is perhaps the best resource, with links to routes, cycle hire and tours.

Cycle hire outlets include **Rijwielshop Rotterdam** (www.czwaan.nl) offering bike rental from the central train station from around 7.50 euro a day, **Cityrent Rotterdam** (www.cityrent.nl) also near the station and hiring a range of bikes to include tandems and e-bikes, and **Kuijper Tweewielers** (www.gebruikte-fietsen.eu) who offer a delivery service.

Some good themed route suggestions for Rotterdam can be found on the "cities" pages of www.holland.com although these are descriptive and lack maps. For more detailed suggestions and maps Fietsen in Regio Rotterdam (www.fietseninregiorotterdam.nl) has a number of varied routes, including themed options, and you can plan your own routes using the route planner – in Dutch only.

Cycle tour operators include **Urban Guides** (www.urbanguides.nl) with a range of themed tours covering the industrial heritage, architecture and culture of the city, and **RO Tours** (www.rotours.nl) offering three key tours: *Big City, City Centre and Architecture.*

Accommodation is varied, with some hotels and hostels offering in house bike hire. Suggestions include **Hostel Rotterdam** (www.stayokay.com) with a bike hire service, **Hostel Ani and Haakien** (www.anihaakien.nl) offering a city location and bike hire, and **Alberti B&B** (www.alberti-bb.nl) which provides guests with the use of a bike!

"Nothing compares to the simple pleasure of riding a bike." John F Kennedy

National tourist routes

Dutch Coastal Route (North Sea Cycle Route)

The Dutch Coastal Route is made up of routes LF1 and LF10 of the national cycle network which in turn make up part of the larger North Sea Cycle Route (www.northsea-cycle.com) or EuroVelo 12 (www.eurovelo.com). The route covers around 570km and is essentially made up of two sections taking you along the coast from Sluis in the South West to Callantsoog along the Noordzee Route (LF1), and then continuing north along the Waddenzee route (LF10) to Nieuweschans. The two sections are distinctly different with the LF1 characterised by long, narrow dune areas, lively coastal resorts and the South Holland and Zealand islands, and the LF10 taking in calm panoramic scenery, farmland and sparsely populated villages as well as passing the Wadden Sea Islands world heritage site.

Picture: from www.holland.com

Key places of interest along the Noordzee route (LF1) include Zoutelande and Westkapelle, collectively known as the Zeeland Riviera. Zoutelande has an unremarkable history, but in recent times has become a popular seaside resort, owing to its sheltered geography, long beaches and high sunshine. Zoutelande also has some of the highest dunes in the Netherlands, reaching up to 54 meters and making them a popular spot for hand gliders.

Further down the coast and around 35km from Rotterdam is the small, little known fortress town of Brielle. Brielle is steeped in history and was a key town during the Eighty Years War as the capture of Brielle by the Dutch Rebells in 1572 signalled the beginning of the Dutch uprising against Spain. The town has a number of prominent architectural features and national monuments, not least the fortress that surrounds the town that has been largely unchanged since 1713.

The town of Callantsoog marks the end of the LF1 section of the Dutch Coastal Route and is another fine coastal resort. The town has been rebuilt several times following coastal flooding, with the construction taking place further inland on each occasion. To the south of

Callantsoog is the Zwanenwater, a diverse nature reserve rich in plants and birdlife well worth a visit.

One of the highlights of the LF10 section of the route is the Lauwersmeer National Park (www.np-lauwersmeer.nl). The fascinating reserve has been gradually growing and developing since the area was dammed in 1969. Now a protected area, the Lauwersmeer National Park has become internationally renowned for its diverse bird and plant life that rely on the specific conditions created by the wet/dry and brackish and freshwater extremes. Of particular importance are the orchids of the area that offer beautiful floral displays in June and July. For cyclists, the area has a dedicated cycle route "Rondje Lauwersmeer" that consists of a 45km circuit covering the various areas of the park.

Accommodation along the Dutch Coastal Route is easy to find and Cyclist Welcome suggestions (from South West to North East) include **De Blikken** campsite (www.deblikken.nl Rian Hoste, Barendijk 3, 4503 GT, Groede); **Strandhotel Bos & Duin** (www.hotelbosenduin.nl Duinweg 82, 4356 GD, Oostkapelle); **Badhotel Rockanje** (www.badhotel.nl Tweede Slag 1, 3235 CR, Rockanje); **Hostel Noordwijk** (www.stayokay.com/nl/hostel/noordwijk Langevelderlaan 45, 2204 BC, Noordwijk); **t Bullekroffie** (www.bullekroffie.nl Korte Ruigeweg 43, 1757 GN, Oudesluis); **Hotel 't Heerenlogement** (www.heerenlogement.nl Franekereind 23, 8861 AA, Harlingen) and Camping Maarlandhoeve (www.campingmaarlandhoeve.nl Havenweg 54, 9981 JR, Uithuizen).

More about Holidays by Cycle

Holidays by Cycle is a Social Enterprise and registered Community Interest Company (CIC) and was initially set up in 2013 to provide a European wide accommodation and cycle hire linking service and establish a business that promoted sustainable travel and less reliance on cars as a means of transport. With the growing popularity of cycling on holiday, the expanding network of routes, the increase in cycle hire outlets, improved integration of rail networks and the growing awareness of "green" issues the formula seemed ideal. As the concept developed, it became clear that cycle tourism in Europe lacked any single point of reference that brought the resources, business and services together to enable people to arrange any level or type of cycle related holiday. Holidays by Cycle is now the only online resource that combines cycle hire, cycle routes, cycle holidays, rail networks and the only European directory of cycling friendly accommodation.

How it works

Holidays by cycle is a resource for every tourist, and aims to simplify the process of integrating cycling into traditional holidays as well as assisting dedicated cycle tourists with their travel plans. From the family who wants to hire bicycles whilst self-catering or book a holiday tour to the serious long distance cyclists who requires cycle friendly accommodation on route - we list all types of cycle friendly accommodation, cycle hire, routes and tours as well as providing useful information so planning a cycling inspired holiday is made simple.

The site is set up to facilitate your own planning on a "do it yourself" basis, or to use the expertise of professional tour providers. Holidays by Cycle is the only website to list cycle friendly accommodation, cycle hire providers and organised tour companies across Europe, as well as providing route suggestion of our own and routes from the Open Cycle Map. If you wish to combine your cycling trip with rail transport, we have also provided transport maps and booking gateways for Rail Europe and The Train Line. Finally, to ensure you are enthused and informed for your cycle trip, we provide useful articles from those in the know. Holidays by Cycle is therefore the complete resource for cycle tourism related information in Europe.

Donate?

As a non profit social enterprise, Holidays by Cycle reinvests any profits back into the business. Also, we donate a percentage of profits to sustainable transport charity Sustrans. To find out more visit: www.holidaysbycycle.com

HOLIDAYS BY CYCLE
THE COMPLETE CYCLE-TOURISM RESOURCE

ISBN-13: 978-1511817981

Holidays by Cycle CIC

11 Woodfield Ave

Wolverhampton

WV4 4AG

Registered Community Interest Company

Printed in Poland
by Amazon Fulfillment
Poland Sp. z o.o., Wrocław